LYDIA UNSWORTH
Yield

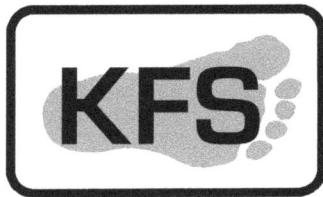

KFS

Newton-le-Willows

Published in the United Kingdom in 2020
by The Knives Forks And Spoons Press,
51 Pipit Avenue,
Newton-le-Willows,
Merseyside,
WA12 9RG.

ISBN 978-1-912211-65-4

Notes & Acknowledgements:

These poems are a call-and-response with the Tao Te Ching, a stretch back and spring forward between, across, and within the texts and my own sensory overload. Mashed together with fragmented lyrics from past Eurovision Song Contest winners and phrases from traditional English-language folk songs, these poems, written over a period of one month, absorbed the daily Tao verse, wrote notes back to it in plain speak, scanned one newspaper article, mined for lyrics from pre-selected laments and love songs, stole a line from the previous day's Tao-poem, and then allowed myself to begin.

These poems were all draft-written as part of the Tupelo 30/30 project in June 2019. I am very grateful for the space and the pace and the community that this platform provided.

Many thanks to the editors at *Pamenar Press*, *Chaudiere Books*, and *Queen Mob's Teahouse*, where some of these poems first appeared.

Thanks also to all my friends, without whom I can't do anything really.

Supported using public funding by
**ARTS COUNCIL
ENGLAND**
LOTTERY FUNDED

For Enrique

CONTENTS

An act of editorship is bound to reflect something of the individual doing the editing: a plaster cast of an aesthetic — not the actual thing, but the imprint of it.

As a work gets more autobiographical, more intimate, more confessional, more embarrassing, it breaks into fragments.

– David Shields, *Reality Hunger*

Outer Play /

You roll out the map to insulate your home. Stapling cloth to the wall is the only way if your heart doesn't want to give in. You staple the end of your sleeve to the corner of a reappropriated patch of curtain, forgetting the day-to-day demands of your arm therein. You roll your body inside out, trying to escape the reassurance of bifurcation, rustling newspapers behind card behind card behind thick old coats once stuffed with the straw we also used to sleep in. You're inside-out now, your arm interlocked with a finite but uncertain number of other limbs, bodies tipping, loop-the-looping, hands in hands in nameless patches of housewear. The goal is to become a slim ring, ironed out, blowing in the redirected wind. The goal is to shrink a bedroom back to the size of the cupboards that render unnecessary the separate bedrooms we alonely used to dream in. Built into the living room, as then as now, closed off during the day. If one day someone asks about me, tell them I'm finally learning to drive. Tell them that up on the moor it isn't even cold. Tell them there's a farm boy in the rear-view mirror holding his cows to account, trying not to let the docile multiply. Tell them to send more clothes.

Beget Each Other /

Oh don't tell the gods I left a mess, tell them to send more clothes instead. Out of the unwashed pile on the floor, I choose the cleanest, sniff the pockets. Exertion is only noticed once we learn to show it. It's a skill to be awake

to which flowers are worth smelling, to know alternative names for things. We say *op*, which means *up*, which means *gone*, which means *where*—and I imagine I'm saying *operation* every time I finish a thing. Casually flinging out the *p*, which seems to happen more and more often since I had the baby. Oh—

one aspires and then closes the hole. We're growing faster than wild roses (as) one by one we queue for the children's slide. It teaches us about size, about the boredom and fascination of a life in time, about letting oneself go.

Quiet Ambition and Strengthen Spine /

Up to no good, the sky is red tonight with no rewards. *If nothing is done, all is gone well,* they cry, casually flinging out the wild roses, stems cut at aggressive angles, undesired vases slicing the fat, loose air. I want to want nothing, to stop stealing treasure from my own safety-deposit boxes like a coin stealthed between two closed hands. Take me to a field of weeds so that I, too, can untether. Wean me on your dominant pronouns so that I, too, only see myself as shades of Smashbox or CoverGirl. Nude as the cream foundation into which I was born. Cracking up like Golconda on a wall. Tracing one warm line through a land so dark, melting a little fire into the chamber pot of what we expected, what was expected of us: that we go on being beautiful and living small.

Untangle /

With one hand in your mouth / and your finger in your eye / you soften the glare of the spilled cocktails on the boulevard tiles / You soften the words lining your tongue before flapping them out on the cool post-puddles.

Cracking up: oil painting in years of light. This is not the average time it takes a person of my age to get their body off the floor. My feet can hold me. My arms can hold. Standing on the edge of a diving board. Potential energy loaded up inside like I want to be your shelter and keep you safe—

Chlorine wharfs between us. The unplanned patterns of displacement meets design.

Much Talk /

I crawled to confession early today. Crept through the half-closed slat to learn my tyres had been slashed. I was on the wrong side of the door. Silent as a sine wave, I corkscrewed to the core of your business ventures, your video conferences, your seasonal promotional pre-packed packages. What I did there was I knocked on the walls—reconstructed, as thought—and the women kept flowing through, following the clear arrows. No one else could make me sadder than a line of you. Then, the nothingness of a Rembrandt I'm told how to enjoy. If you drop your wife in a car park, spin her round three times, and make a run for it, you can paint what you like. The routines of cleaners will get her body off the concrete. They'll water the flowers, feed the stags tied to the lampposts. Polish the laminated heads of the many missing animals. There are tiny factors sterilising all the surfaces. We move, we yield, sucking up and spitting out hairs.

Doors and Windows /

Loops of inefficiency stir us tighter together in spaghetti-inhale. I can't even notice the real world when virtually every object in the sky has more than one designation. They'd always just been there. Stars like gasps of not, without which, a Messier fullness. Eighty-seven spokes join the rim to the hub, and it's habitable for now. They'd always just gone there. I'm told how to enjoy the many missing animals like a bowl made from clay that we wouldn't be able to use if so much of the sphere hadn't already been extracted from the ball. They're calling for the bans to end because some like it raw—some like it shot. The pathetic flicker of a new moon. You don't know who's coming back, and that, you think, is the benefit of living in the city, that surprise, that waiting for it, that bubble you create only to have it bought.

Seasoning /

Liquid beds silently expand the way ivory stockpiles, the way the balloon wouldn't burst however many times you bounced on it and I kept saying it would because,

as we would see, I was wrong. You keep bouncing anyway; only you can know what your body demands. The bluebell hangs its drooping head as if to focus on itself. The only treasure I'll ever have is ~~the functioning of my~~

is

is you until you're gone. Raw leaves, even spinach—all worryingly wild.

The idea of letting anything inside, even light. Some like it raw, without any kind of seasoning. Plain rice absorbing water like tears let down into pillows in the night. The threat of anything but us trying to take back land.

Some people have booming elephant populations they'd rather not come into contact with. Can't sell them on because people without elephants are telling people with too many elephants what to do with their elephants:

it's not on. I say do what your belly tells you, look in, not out. Firmly insert the magazine. The elephants can take care of themselves. Don't be shy. Take what you need, not what you want.

Goat /

Nothing in the world that could stop me rising—the way a source of meat rises plucked from an open flame.

I won't spend hours deciding what to wear; the word *heel* frightens me, puts me in my place.

I want to trample over 7,000 hectares of your crops, take what I need. It is only because I have a body that I am seen.

On the television, you present my fat childhood that others might learn. The lip-clench away-glance of my nationally broadcast resignation becomes prime-time regime. *Trust her.* Heavy clods in the thinning air.

Let someone who doesn't give a damn about us give a damn about us. Two accidental arms flung backwards to see what they can reach. Disco-ball facets in their million-fold stare. The hardest thing to re-s-train is a long *oh-o-oohhh* and to keep that surge of feeling from feeling like our mistake.

These Three Qualities (Null Set) /

Every night's a Friday night because the music in us will never mutate. We've been told to listen, but I've turned and turned and I can't hear a sound beyond the string of mirrors expanding what little available light. My own voice rang out from underneath the pillow: *Apparently*. Woke me up, a word so bright. Ladies, this sure feels right. I'm collapsing into Soho on a Saturday power-outage. Air so thin I'm doused in what might yet permeate; contactless, going off people's given names, where their hearts begin to pump so same so same. Standing by the growth chart, nothing's changing, nothing at all. What night? I only register as taller when the rule falls off the wall. Call it excitatory if you like, a word that itself peaked around 1999. I can't be pinned down, seen, explained. On the glowing squares it becomes important to know the history of dancing. The history of drink. Still, we believe we were made to laugh and sing.

Old Masters /

Valley-dip of evening   and loose loud clink of corner chair in crowded
blue. Is there room enough for two? For two more halves? Joy only costs a day's
pay and if we meet before night is over then I'll be granted a step,
a stoop,
stupor.
→ Stupid ← Too pissed to frighten myself out of the room. We're on the bottleneck
of a mountain ridge that guaranteed my former self the return leg to—

    was promised air.
             My foot in
                my sock
                    in my shoe
                        only wants what it's entitled to.

The sketch of a descent. More expensive flights again. The people here who
really want it.
And no more.

    Who is
whole? I was a whole thing in the blanket—sharing this, shaking something,
going limp and then slowly stirring up a life. We can't be pinned down:

        deft and subtle as populist rhetoric. Keep banging that drum till the
neighbours appear,
            and then,
self-effacing,
face them.

                      We chase litter down the street,
                      blowing in the angry minefield.
                      We're jumping to catch a strip
                      of blue and silver tape: is this
    car.   plastic? We're unsure. Trying
            car.

                      so hard not to get hit by a passing

This is thought to be
a late interpolation /

Empty as real estate, the moon shines fairly in an undeveloped dawn. I try to stand still but the motorbikes are going round and through me. Severing my small intensity with their crude virtue, unhelmeted horsepower slick like oil. If the hat fits, I'll buy it—sometimes a thing doesn't happen twice. Stay empty or you will be rendered so: stripped of atmosphere, bland as punishment. Tie your shoelaces to the nuts and bolts of the ground and, pinned down, let your body blow about there. You are safe if you are slow, grand if you can secure land. Shine a light in every corner of my heart; my lungs are chocked with petrochemicals, despite what the underlying lichen would prefer, so don't stray far. Stay, like the baggy clouds, keep me from looking up at everything I will bludgeon, crack open, and allow to die. Come back to haunt me with your nothing-cannot-haunt spiel, with your space where a word should be. Yearn for silence? Embrace this: a zoo without a z, a mars without an ours, a moon we shouldn't own. My active fingers twitch. To buy is to cope, to handle. I want to exchange stock, forge bonds, divvy up the yield. An empty shelf is a dusty shelf, a source of respiratory hardening. It's not my vault. Reapportion what you want, but not blame, not here. I'm not trying to frighten you, I'm just trying to make you agree.

Lost Faith Breeds /

Regret spills out into public domain. At first the leader isn't noticed; then the five stages of grievance. Podium warfare silly-dancing into all our hearts—like a first love, if we had one, if we convinced ourselves of the piano among the dahlias behind the fringe of trees. *Mama* is a word I would prefer not to notice, so often am I wet up to the kneecaps, adorned with filth, striking at the striking transport for the inconvene. Once adored—then coil, then knife, ignore. Then lose. Let loose. The darkness had to leave. Although I'm mud and gory spattered, I've gathered all my offspring. We're pitching our tent and leaving no trace by the side of the water. And you can't say you personal-assisted, you can't say any single motion was either fated or natural. Hail effluvia, I'm moved—shame not to be. Banking on finding the right full mood.

Managers and the Managed /

Suddenly an open door, said the lionfish to the lionfish at the biopsied neck of the Suez canal. Remove the cyst, sister; our springboard fins have come home to this beautiful land! Like when your head fills up with the same thought over and over (in one nostril and out the other) so the lionfish expands. The seabed drains into default auto. Fashions change. I stepped over two soon-to-be-not-long-dead-bodies on the way to a life's work this morning. Couldn't do a thing about it. The queue said *Go on.*

I've never been this close, I whispered to the Sherpa who had photocopied my passport. Leaving no trace, she took my heart rate and diminished up the hill with my fast lost blood on her over-gloved hands. Never had a skirt fit me so well. Never had I seen a thing happening to my body and been at one with it. Sedentary, sedated: fetch the osteopath, the chiropractor. Hemorrhaging last-chances like a long-bored couple killing everything within sight two times a week. *I said it,* I told them as the committee gathered to put their trust in legislation, *but I did not say it well.*

(Grasp at) Externals /

Trust in legislation/the seabed, empty your pockets and pause by the security camera and say *not yet*. When it's Richter-scale in my heart I turn to hypha— determined downward twitches that apologise while gaining ground. Fingers in alcoves of loose skin, bleach-garbed manipopulations dribbling a hundred ways to sling a country further into the ring. Let me out by the estuary, thanks. Tie me to the cliff on the west side of the island, pink ribbons in my hair. Guide me to the silo. Silence. Send me sliding down the shapely side of the nuclear power plant, crisp eyes tearing up as my property flies out of my open bag and over my control. When I die, leave me in a sun-roofed sinkhole, fondue to your foundations, and tear my stolen stillhouse down.

So Sometimes Ahead and Sometimes Behind /

On the out-of-action travelator I enjoy the hum of suitcase wheels rotating around. Various degrees of metal, plastic—grating. In the vibrations of my active life, the smell of failure, what remains of the countryside, your cold light. A long thread of recognisable hair that ties me to a sound.

The words came low and mournfully from the loudspeaker: *I don't think anyone can.* And a fantastic range of fragrances swallowed the social animal whole.

We prepare to land like duffel bags of instant grief dropped from altitude: ample, one square metre apart. Squatting in formation on the sand we relieve ourselves, are relieved, dawn dawns on us, sudden and bright as our gashes of open eyes, alerting around. We live in a state of indecision, not yet certain enough to admit that inaction is not the same as deciding not to. Pinning our rained-on bodies to the tongued-up ground. Caught between doing and undoing, resting between sentences like being too scared to enter a room.

My chin rests, babyshape, on our suitcase handle, until it chews on the lever and drop-darts down. Tears drip like unfamiliar showers in a land you were once accustomed to, as you fly towards the year 2000 looking for the point of departure: trawling for scraps of asymptote rainbow gold,

until the snapped elastic sends you back through to your opposite bullet hole. Everything is contained in the pillow of another's shoulder, in the narrow strip of sea that tells our houses to face the water. Sunlight sparks mosquito swarms into trying to grab anything with your razor-blade hands of a person. Observe the wires and contact points and closed-up circuits, cut a line through skin and look around. Telephone boxes have a place in my heart. Sometimes, a start, a control.

Get It Over With /

Plastic-wrapped humps of landfill sprout parks, base layer, something on which to build. Polyamorous as my ten little fingers, the confetti swaggers its clutch into submarine loads. Tease a tassel through the impermeable (unavoidable) eventual (regrettable) hole—beauty finds a way, kitsch, a vulgar display. The gas will out of its venus-flower-basket home. It was the knowledge I wanted, but now my attic's so full that the ceiling dips down. We say, *disorder in the streets,* but I, too, am a piece of traffic. You've simply got to start hotting up and not telling anybody about it. Covert little cakes, sugar grains spilling out from the flaps of your unbought clothes. I see people bend their backs as if a life is worth nothing. We're not paid to dance. There's no choice but to carry on talking, force out a little slack. Let the words come low and boil around your melting toes.

Fine Weapons (an unfitting) /

Saw in the morning with a wet kiss. Slid over sleep like the promise of snow did. Grabbed you lion-shape on the floor and told your body to grow, like a daffodil. I do not have a fortune to buy you pretty things. Do not have the stamina to chase your breakneck thrill. You too can hate weapons, if you give up the drink. Splat like a storm-leaf, I mean, darken, fill. Never say *pregnant with*. And the water in your eyes found its way into mine, because a river, casual, will wend a route to its prize. Imagine an obstacle, for example, a comb, a calculator, fear of lightning, three men in the night. And now imagine a leak. Loud as a tooled-up father, toiled-out after Time spent keeping it in. The starling-bomb cloud, the one that flies over, leaves a nightclub of sky on the blind of your eye. The ceiling sinks down from all the electricity it is currently holding and the night won't stop taking my photograph, screaming at me to resign.

Nobody's Serve /

Enduring averages collapse under weight. A lifelong abstinence says sorry, says sorry again. I will teach you anything but theologies, chagrin. If everyone could fall low, the world would be perfect with no sky and we would be able to touch each other's things without ruining them: dropped glass wouldn't break.

A transparency is conceived to fragment.

As for my father, in his tower, throwing his unwashed washing down the communal rubbish chute; I told him we couldn't hang our clothes out to dry anymore, not in Rome, not in any of your interchangeable knots of carbon. You see, everywhere was full, and that symptom of outsideness, that exoskeletal display, it wouldn't end up anywhere good, and those vests and knickers would just become another garbled Wikipedia page saying maybe criminal, maybe cultural—

and maybe it is enacted over the whole of this insert-timezone, but we're not looking up in case the knee-jerk takes our eye out. And all the crumpled garments lay loose-limbed on the floor. And we're sorry we didn't dig this city because under every metro station was another little hole waiting to be filled.

The one that flies over can stay where it is; I'm not asking for a plane to trail a banner into all this anyway cloudfall. I am just a girl who says what she feels, who picks up indiscriminate after-objects on the beach, who still turns her head a touch too quickly if somebody calls her (a) name.

Force Serves /

Ending a day is the hardest, that much we're born into. Shouting *help* across proto-thumbs as we dim the lights. You look down on the ground to find the next thing we'll be requiring: a bracelet, a toy car, the lesson a dead-bodied sparrow lets drop from loose indoors. As I said, don't let your indecision take you from behind. After which, we stepped into the funicular, expecting rice fields, steppe, alpine shards, and receiving instead a diminishing dark, the excavation of a town. Taught us a thing or two, the ride, how to put the fun in punctual, how to overcome the underground (mole-like, with half-closed eyes), how you can't bypass anything in a week, not even with purpose, purchase. It's the traffic islands I want to cling to, those abundant, uncontested no-drive zones around which high-speed disappearance swings. Persist like a fingernail persists, like an ant underfoot persists carrying another ant upon its middling thorax. Love life, take it by the home. I pitched my tent in the estuary to be delivered archetypically into the open mouth.

It does its work /

If I were a featherbed, saved up from the leftovers of how I used what came, I'd sag soft atop your cool firm base. Unindulge me with a single word, flamboyant dash on my curl-cruel fist shape. Undone like too much looking at who's afraid in a public space. Down a certain path you see a certain owl, a certain boy punches a certain woman against the corrugated cardboard of this small business is closing down. You do not intervene properly, but later begin to walk through the built-up park at the switch of night, expectant, anonymously exposed. I want to say armour, but it's harm rather, a manner of protesting the prideless allocation of your time and (personal) space. Hallelujah, says the park gate when another body finds the threshold to another paltry escape. Flesh is to leaves as a slip hazard is to an open grave. All over it, the park sprouts clappy yellow bivalves of preventative danger: *wet floor, wet floor.*

The World Comes to You /

Nowhere I could go that could be more coast than this. And what do you want when you get there? I can give you a thing—a patchwork, thousands of precious names that the tide will take away, and if I dull my eyes the whole of the sand gently phosphoresces a retreat. We talk, but I see you see what is left of my fingers, and I grasp the formless form, that is, the gulf (gulp) that lies (dare I?) between us, and what I want is thick and fast and full of guts and lust and anything congealed enough to be called stuff and what you want from life is fine and certainly isn't mine, but I came (pause) and you came (paused)—

She who sees birds flying away has eyes for the prize but hands for the light brush of an unattended shawl, intending to speak but instead swiping the ruff of the differences between us. I lie (sigh) down upon your double resort and wait and wait as the water encrusts the trunk of my (is there any other word for it?) body, each lap of tide an amateur (age-old) manner of protesting (testing). I am hurt (broken) amplified (leave it) each time anyone (anyone) (wait) (!) walks.

Leave the Fish in the Deep /

Growth hormones push through the ground; give a girl a cuttlefish and see what comes out. If you're one of those people concerned about germs, then put your headphones on and stay away from the airport. Be careful near the edge of the boat, a strong wind, loose shards, a stalk of gulls—never flapping, always the same distance, gusto. To be permanent you have to move, hips wobble as you reacquaint with hard-boiled land. Gills, wings,

you'll be trampled in the tumult. A hovering cloudlet is seen like an apocalypse, heavy and predictable, a shade of monster quick to be disrespected: it'll never touch us. What does?

We are repellent to our neighbours. The side mouth, the trying-to-be-neutral eyes. Agents of holiday death, a lighthouse, a light. We float, we know we float, I have dropped goods into the wetness and witnessed. Shallow, we stick to the shallows where the sand in the water sometimes

splinters the sky. Try to smile while you say goodbye, stiff lips won't reveal the shore, a shaking hand, the clots of origamied life. I'm a row of boats: arrow-thin masts, flaring matchsticks. And the endeavour of never wrapping around a cell, a planet. The moon is the biggest of all the stars: nearby, unknown, a tyrant.

If Desire Stirred I'd Bury It /

You say I sleep like a log, sunburnt and with all the outer layers peeling off. I say I'm letting the world do what it wants. There's no time for preventative measures, not since the dreams of the artist were auctioned off. Sold to the lovers we might find in the compound, if only we'd go and say goodbye, finish them off, stand atop the last remaining tower and stamp our feet as the frames come rollicking down. Be careful what you say after you've passed a place, your words can no longer be held up against it, no longer the soft *e,* the heady *s,* dialect has died and left us. What I'm saying is international, passionate, if only the governors could grasp it. Slowly the everything I've ever been immersed in. Slowly the missed mist and our eventual rejuvenation. Slowly missile. Firing its blank pages. And the plaque in the waiting room that says mistakes are only changes we haven't yet made. The undone hangs from the ends of my shoelaces, free until it settles into *amarcord.*

Like This So Near /

One who prefers to walk is a liability next to all the cars. *It's nearly always half a day to water,* drivers scream from their rolled-down dust-scuffed window guards. I missed the bus on purpose to again feel scale. I've got my phone, wallet, sunhat, suncream, map of the known world (tracked, trapped, sleek in my short-trouser pocket). I've got keys to an apartment, shoes, access to food, a bench, a tree, a street to trace. The best state is small, from such a position you can only be favoured, teased, coerced up into this wild life. From there you are given gestures, a lap, common ground, dress sense, grace. Learn to weave, to revive, reveal. Fields are knocked back to make way for the roads. I know how to tack a rug to a wall, I know what it's for, but right now (slowly missile) I am slipping into this train   \to be carried/   on one last sojourn.

Therefore, Look /

Universe is slopes of heather-purple guffaw, is a row of houses curving upwards into the centre of a good strong mount. Clouds sweep like a stealth of cleaners; frail collected wisps disintegrate like the ends of sentences boomeranged out into too-large halls. Come on, let us foot it out of here together, real as crops, tall grass in our eyes and sails. Arms roving, pounding away the long trails of bipedal life between us and the lie the land fielded. Firm means firm, blades crouch low and wait to regain. The nation prospers, while we, knocking back the grain blocking the soon-to-be-ferocious thoroughfare, have so little other than each other to try and say to our assailants. Loud in my ear grew the people, the town stretched maternal over my full face. What is mine is yours: duplicitous relay. Universe, looked at, cannot slip away.

Whatever Is Contrary Will Not Last Long /

Rail against the iron rusting in summer rain. Unpounced on, this newborn before the close of the first day. High-moral bar of fresh-faced human lets animals know to forge their own safe state. This wasn't for dealing out, this freehold, wasn't supposed to be such a small enclave. I'd banked on it, shrank, sunk into the plush of cushion cover and dreamy beige. Velvet upholstery, idyllic curtains, that forever un-ness that allows you to wrap yourself around a slender dining chair and tremble. Unspent energy like a building being built, like a runaway runway, like a fork of lightning in the splitting road, like grinding new teeth into wannabe vultures pecking local exposures into wannabe souls. Only strong enough to go on shouting until it turns itself into un-noteworthy stranglehold. I'm saying bob along, the surface ponders only the tension of the oil-slick licking the bird wings sticking to the thickness of that same spilled surface. Reclaim a little wasteland. A slow breath without mention, a gathering momentum. A trick. The ends are taught to meet; meaning we're all one thing. But we didn't start the swing, the metronome stands tall at the arse-end of the inner ring road. Cull, culpable, the silent sabbatical man who, on the retour, raised the volume to unsafe levels and sang, unquiet, his silent sabbatical song.

Temper your Sharpness /

Small victory to have learned this dogfight. The debate is scheduled for cancellation—if half the fight stays home the fight can't go on. At night, under the hook of the collapsed tree, plates can be heard, furniture, screeching to a halt. The desire to go back to the wild, sing in the morning with how to start slow. Taking calls from the phone lane while getting-one's-pedometer-on. She was something in her day, and now at thirty-three, like a side dish sliding down the long table leg of dining out, she's learning the vocabulary of how to set her place. You're a coward if you don't harp on. Record me recording the palm on the platelets. Stand up, on trembling legs, quit nursing, rehearsing, stand up and be a man. To not be seen is also seen as a sign of weakness, let's get this party started, you've no business buying a mare like that, go on you must go on.

Who knows what the future holds? /

Examples of the city are laid on thick. We look at the earth from the side of the boat as it drifts goodbye, goodbye, goodbye from the bank of waiters serving up the haven, all kitted out in limestone frill. I'm all about leaving if you do it quick. Tell me how to moderate, to become moderate, and I'll spread my limbs out over the decking, sew up my old clothes, and create a clean sheet. I want to lie like a thin film, almost nothing yet inescapable, almost nothing yet every time you breathe in. I've been to the city and I know it's not for me. But I will not leave. Hard to say no to a puddle of affirmity. To an infinity pool that just won't quit. Drown me in your middle-ground while the seven seas are swollen, sold, solid, stolen. Lined with overturned cheeks. The lines were drawn in charcoal, pastel; we thought nothing of it at the time, but it did not rain, would not rain. (We would be the last (at last (we will not last)).) We wouldn't let it.

Principle of Ruling /

Lowlands pull on my underwater heart. You say the salt sea will repent until it drowns us all. Distance, distilled, turns into art: intimate, hundreds of us, coddled in grief. I care, of course, I can care from anywhere, anytime, make of me what you will. Giving up against a long line of trees, the sweat pours out, sapping your strength, what you had left of it, willowing, withering, in the plainness of the remaining weather, trunk bulging in the high street's AC wind. Head coppiced into stubborn knot. I attack the podium, fist-bump the event organizers. I am young, I do not need to fall in love with any old thing. The past, as we report it, is now tasteless, now largely water. We dream of the Mediterranean, of a real tomato. Having been so good for so long. If the past serves, nothing is unattainable. If you have a past, you can rule a nation with a certain girth: we say depth, death, dearth. The door won't close. Once you're in you're in.

We Will Not Hurt One Another /

For the umpteenth time I turned my face away
and danced in the darkest coolest corner. Bold
in the kernel of voice-activated self-shade.

A fight is not a fight when nobody protests it.
An altercation, a tucked-in shirt,
one hand over another, a sunny-side cloudburst.

Shoulders warm beneath flung arms, a dart from one
to not a moment too soon. Stylish dresses overmoon
the flattened grass of an island
in heat; we're in the shadows, still hiding
slightly, still learning to meet. I'm dancing and
dancing in remembered acquaintance, in the surface blue swoon
that takes breath away (a moment too soon). A hand passes;

I tell it to write me a long, long letter.
Spill and the world will spill with you,
dip your feet in the water, allow your torso to wade
into fond skin and quickly
blame refraction, the afternoon. My face, moist,
imprisoned, personal, familiar. And my hands:
mattress-blunt, awkward shifting blankets. A doily falls

through the break between two lined-up tables, a detail caught
on a million elsewhere heels and then abandoned. The breeze is still
the breeze in this furnace-grill daylight. I'm curtain-caught
in the billowy folds of everyone leaking out
of the thrown-wide and forget-your-woes windows.
An orchard pops open another bottle. Clouds cheer
into spontaneous dissipation—into fill and be filled.

Speak and the world won't know how to refuse.